EBURY PRESS

DREAMING WITH MY EYES WIDE OPEN

Joey Kidney is a creator, author, mental health advocate and entrepreneur. He began posting on YouTube in 2012 after he broke his leg during a hockey game. He had already suffered several concussions due to the sport, but in 2012, he decided to put his unfortunate circumstance to good use.

Joey saw almost immediate success posting weekly videos on YouTube, until he amassed a 7,00,000-subscriber base. He later found his way over to TikTok, gaining over 5.2 million followers and a new audience hungry for his content. He has 9,95,000 followers on Instagram, a large number of which are from the Indian subcontinent.

Joey highlights his journey, navigating the highs and lows of mental health, adulthood, being a dog dad and purchasing his first home most recently. He began writing his life story in 2017 and published his first book, *What's the Rush?*, in 2019. In 2021, he wrote his first poetry book, *Dreaming with My Eyes Wide Open*.

Joey has released several songs with Milestone, a collaboration with Matt Walden, gaining over 10 million plays on Spotify.

He has followed up *What's the Rush?* with *Take Your Time & Hurry Up*, which starts the next day, and continues documenting his life through the ups, downs and everything in between.

DREAMING WITH MY EYES WIDE OPEN

JOEY KIDNEY

EBURY
PRESS

An imprint of Penguin Random House

EBURY PRESS

USA | Canada | UK | Ireland | Australia
New Zealand | India | South Africa | China | Singapore

Ebury Press is part of the Penguin Random House group of companies
whose addresses can be found at global.penguinrandomhouse.com

Published by Penguin Random House India Pvt. Ltd
4th Floor, Capital Tower 1, MG Road,
Gurugram 122 002, Haryana, India

Penguin
Random House
India

First published by Stay You LLC dba Stay You Press 2021
This edition published in Ebury Press by Penguin Random House India 2024

Acknowledgments

I owe the world and more to Maria for bringing this book to
life through the awe-inspiring images that she has created.
I am always truly amazed by her work. Thank you!

Artist: Maria Melito

I may make words sound good, but sometimes I use the wrong ones.
Very thankful to have Nicki to correct me and be so supportive.

Editor: Nicki Richards

ISBN 9780143463917

For sale in the Indian Subcontinent only

Printed at Replika Press Pvt. Ltd, India

www.penguin.co.in

MIX
Paper from
responsible sources
FSC® C016779

Dedication

I am constantly caught dreaming with my eyes open during the day because the nighttime is when my mind is most awake. Taking in every single possibility of how my life could be or how it will play out as if I know the answer to either. Stuck in my head as I walk around this world looking at things, being in places, and loving with people. I am in this other world that I created in my head that seems to be so peaceful yet terrifying at the same time. I close my eyes and it all seems to go away, but when I open them, the world tends to blend with the reality that I am living in right now.

This may make a hell of a lot of sense to some and it may confuse a lot more, but I am not writing this for you to understand. I am writing this for you to know that your feelings are valid. Agree or disagree with this concept or false reality that I am describing; the way you interpret this book is solely based on you—where you are, what you are doing, the people you have in your life, and how you hold yourself. There is no one person who can change the way that you feel, because at the end of the day you are the only person who can actually feel those feelings.

This poetry book is for anyone who feels and at the same time anyone who doesn't feel at all.

You're not alone.

-j

A Man's Best Friend

The feeling of being lost
Can be quite lonely

The cancelled plans last minute
The nights that have a limit
And the times when our heart isn't in it

Until someone comes along
And fills the dark void
With a little light

We say we can't trust anyone
But the moment I feel your presence
Is the moment I truly feel joy

The only difference is
He has four paws and a tail

Old Friends

Don't waste your time on people who aren't current

The Hardest Part

The hardest part wasn't letting go
It was trying to understand that you didn't want to stay

One Year

To go to sleep to wake up to someone you love
To have tears fall with someone to catch them
To tumble to the ground with a hand to pull you up

Love isn't always about the morning coffees together
Or the midnight knocks on the door

But rather the shattered hearts that were left on the floor
It is about finding someone whose broken pieces
Fit with yours

Socks & Coffee

When I think about happiness
I think about the times I take a cold shower

And slip on my socks with no friction
Because my feet are completely dry

When I think about happiness
I think about the perfect iced latte

One that cools my chest
And fills my heart with spirit

When I think happiness
I think about me
All the times I got back up
And all the times I stayed down

Because life isn't always about the ups and downs
It is about enjoying where you are
And allowing yourself to frown

Leading with a Faulty Heart

Why wrap me around your finger
When you could wrap me in your arms

Leaving me without a single word
All my thoughts and emotions left unheard

You let me cry without someone to hold
You let me beat without a heart
You let me live without purpose

The least you could do
Is give me a reason

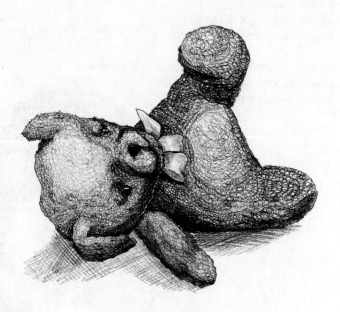

Pain

Your pain was my pain, but mine was never yours

To Whom Didn't Last Forever

It started on the swings
But ended with a sound of rusty chains

We started off better than ever
You were the person I thought
I could swing with forever
But eventually you changed

You moved on in life
And I got left behind

You disappeared without a word
Who knew that a simple "hey"
could leave me so unheard

In Search for Someone to Love

When you are in search for someone to love
Don't come running to me
Because
I will end up falling in love with you
And you will end up leaving me

The Heartbroken Pause

I got my heart broken at the same time
that I told you I loved you
Because I poured out my heart and soul
And you paused...

But(t)

I poured it all out
My heart, my feelings, my soul
And I left it in your hands

Explaining how in love with you I was
Your body, your heart, your love, your butt
And you left me with
"I love you too...but"

I guess spelling does matter

Watching You Fall in Love with Someone Else

When your heart breaks, you are left with broken pieces
on the floor
When the one you love leaves, you hope some of their pieces
will break too

Watching You Walk Away

You think watching you leave was easy?
You think it wasn't hard watching you walk out that door?
You think all I did was go sleep around
To be later yelled at for being a whore?

Then maybe you never really loved me at all
Because if you did
Then none of these things would cross your mind
And I understand thinking of me as the devil
Made it easier to cross that line

To move on, to become the better you

But if you really knew me
Then you'd know that since you walked out that door
I haven't stopped loving you

Leaving You

When I think about leaving you
I think about how hard it was to walk away
I think about how I knew you wouldn't move on
I think about how your love for me would never go astray

But I needed to move on
And in order to do that, I had to hate you
Even though it isn't who you are
I knew you wouldn't go out to a bar
And take home the next boy you saw

Because I knew that the next person to fall in love with you
Would be the luckiest one in the world
And I hated that
Not because I didn't want you to be happy, I did
I just wanted you to be happy with me, because I still loved you

My Version of Love

Love is saying hello without a kiss
Love is saying goodbye without the three words
Love is knowing that they are there
And never feeling unheard

Love is being understood without having to speak
Love is the warmth in their arms
Love is everything you ever dreamed of
But the complete opposite of it

Because love is different for each of us
It comes and it goes so easily
But the pieces that remain
Are the ones that make you feel fulfilled

The Come Back

I could never let you go
No matter how many times I yell it at the top of my lungs
No matter how many times I try to walk away
I'll always come back because I'm here to stay

Beautiful Day

It's such a beautiful day out today,
there's nothing that could be bad about it.
The sun was shining, there were no clouds in the sky
because they were all in my head.

Distanced Love

Love travels a long way
It can make the distance
You just have to want to

Together

The one thing about sadness
That seems to be so peaceful
Is that for once in my life

I don't feel alone
Because I know
That everyone has their moments
When they don't feel strong

The times when they feel like they can't carry on
Are the same times when I feel comfort
Because I know
We've been feeling the same all along

Speechless

I'm out of words to say
Because I've been saying them
in my mind all day

Little Things

I think it is time we start
Being thankful for all the little things
Because one day you will wake up
Not strong enough to handle the big ones

Better Off

I am happy for you
I truly am

I am actually the best I have ever been
And it is because of you

The amount of times that you didn't show up
All the horrible things that you made me feel
And all the moments where I didn't feel loved back

You helped make me who I am today
But in the worst way possible
So don't take this as a thank you

But take it more as a fuck you,
Because I am doing better
Than I ever was
When I was with you

If I Have A Baby Girl

If I have a baby girl
I will want her to be strong

If I have a baby girl
I will want her to be brave

If I have a baby girl
I will want her to come home

With no tears down her face
And no nightmares to try and sleep through

I want to hear about the boy who gave her butterflies
Not about the one that took them away

I have this dream every so often
Of a baby girl running into my arms

Jumping out of happiness, not out of fright
Crying tears of joy and no pain in sight

I dream about this girl every night
And every memory seems to be so happy

But when I take a step outside
And watch all the men pass by

I notice every head turn
as a girl walks by

Doesn't matter the age, or the attire
If you're a girl, their eyes will never get tired

When I think about having a baby girl
I dream about the times she's on the swing

And every dream comes with a soundtrack of her laughter
Hearing her giggles and seeing her smile
But I never looked beyond that

Not noticing a man in the background wearing a hat
On those late-night walks down the street
I am never worried about the people that I might meet
Because as a man I never had to worry about that

But as a girl your head is on a swivel

And as the father I have yet to become
It is not my job to stand in her way
Because women don't need a man to tell them they are strong
As they have been harassed in public and acted like nothing is
wrong

So I am here to stand with her
And not for her
I am going to raise her well
Teach her to stand tall
No matter how many times she falls

And any boy that leaves her crying
My message to her is key
Never let someone stand in the way
Of who you're trying to be

I hope one day you find these words
And take what you need, and take it to heart.
Because I want you to know that you if you
are my daughter
You will never be left unheard

Don't Pick Up a Flower

You should never pick up a flower
If you are just going to play with it
Just let it keep growing

In Another Life

When we look into the future
We look at a better and happier life
The sun shines a different shade
Without a cloud in the sky

Everything seems to be so clear

Another life tends to seem so peaceful
Less worries and less heartbreak
No pain in sight and no hurt in mind

That is, until we get to the thought
That this may have been our other life
This was everything we hoped for
And dreamed of

Everything just became so unclear

Shadows

The sun leaves us a reminder
Of someone we used to be

The past is fading as the world turns
And life continues on

And so should we

Pandemic

Minds racing and billions panicking
All at once
The world finally stopped

And I finally felt caught up

From chasing a world that was spinning too quickly
I could breathe with ease
Walk without sprinting
And love without rushing

When the whole world was crying together
I felt loved

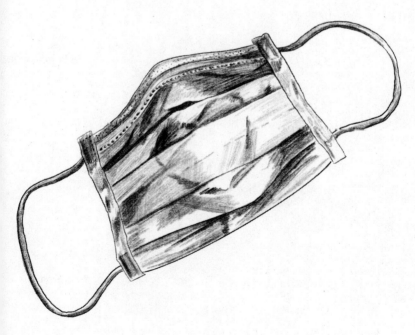

Leaving Me

It's not because you left me
It's because this entire time
I've been waiting

When you left me
You never even looked back

Heartbreak

When you break up with someone
They don't ever feel the same way

That person has just accepted
That you never wanted them
And they will hold that hurt
To their heart forever

Tequila & Lime

Moving on from someone you love
Is similar to a shot and chase

Grab the tequila to numb the pain
Suck the lime to ease the pain

And when you are out of limes
Over time you get used to how it feels
The numbness, the burn, and the discomfort

It leaves you forgetting how painful
It used to be

Change

A line that we have heard many times
"Change is inevitable"
What we all know but never rests easy in our minds

As we grow and move on with life
So does our heart and body
But sometimes our brain is left behind

Missing the moments when life was so simple
There was no pimple to pop or boy to like
It was a life we could always imagine

But as we get older the line comes back again
"Change is inevitable"
And it is a thing we will never need to approve of
Because it is happening anyways

Flashbacks

Every sip of coffee
Every breath of smog
Every bright light
And fast-moving car

I get reminded of all the times we had
And the memory doesn't seem so far

Tea

I am fully convinced that tea slows down the mind
Be careful not to drink too fast, as you may burn your tongue
Relax because if your hand shakes, you may spill your drink

Wait too long, steeped too much
Wait too little, and you have dirty water

I think we should all drink tea
Because it reminds us to slow down
I get flashbacks of the memories in my head
When I am trying something new for the first time
And I am scared to mess up

The butterflies floating in my stomach
My eyes drying out because I refuse to blink
Tea allows us to stop and take a moment to think

And even though it may just be a drink
I feel my heart beat slower after each and every sip

Peace In Sadness

Please be quiet
You are entering a place of peace
The human in the corner may be sad
But they are taking the moment to recharge

Be happy they are here

Saying Goodbye

I never got the chance to say goodbye
You ran out that door years ago
And I remember every lie

You told me you would stay
And that everything would be all right
Yet, I am left here crying
And you are having the time of your life

Reflections

Looking in the mirror and seeing someone you love
Seems to be so impossible
But what if we remove our sight
And base it off of feel

Go a day, a week, and a month without looking in the mirror
And go every second with feeling love

Looks are subjective
So know how you feel
Before asking how you look

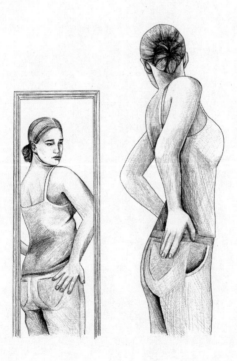

Body Love

Fat or skin and bones
No matter the weight, the world tends to hate

Sweat dripping down our face
Or grease soaking up our pizza

We will never get to where we want to be
When we are working to please
Someone other than ourselves

S**** Happens

A painful emotion when doing something improper
Making you want to disappear from who you once were
And who you are meant to be

When we make mistakes in our life
We forget that in order to get there
Even more mistakes were made prior
Because we learn from trial and error

We love from being unloved
And we learn from our mistakes
Shame happens

Missing Home

I used to think that home was in your arms
It was the place where I always felt welcomed

But I never realized

That when you let me go
I would fall so easily

Happy Place

A spot in my mind
Rather than on this Earth

A place that I would rather be
Than to watch this world burn

Maybe one day
We will realize this world's worth

First Love

The first love is always hard to forget
From the moment you walked in that door
To when you slammed it in my face

No matter how shattered
You will always rest in my heart
In a very precious place

A Different Kind of Love

Love varies with different people
The memories may blend in my head
But sometimes our hearts don't

You can't force love
You can only force the feeling of being wanted.

To My Lost Self

Your head is on a swivel
As if you lost what you're looking for

Up, left, down, right
As if you think it's in plain sight

But what you refuse to acknowledge
Is that you never left who you are

You just started looking
For someone you were never meant
To become.

Pretend You Are Okay

It is about the smile
Nothing more than the smile
Real or fake

It is something that is in question

Surrounded by people with similar pain
Yet we feel alone
And that we have nothing to gain

All I want is to smile
And mean it

I don't remember the last time
I have seen a real one

Alone in Loneliness

I never thought I'd be the one to feel lonely
I figured I would bounce back
Into the midst of it all

But when I wake up in the morning
And look at myself in the mirror
I don't see anyone

I miss seeing someone
I miss feeling something

Absent Presence

You talk about me like I was here
Even when I am trying everything to be present.

Guilty Love

I fear that one day
My guilt will catch up to you
And you will feel all the love
I haven't given you

To My Ex

This isn't about a boyfriend
Or finding someone new

This is about you being so damn happy
That you finally found you

I'm Free

I thought letting you go
Would be the hardest thing
I'd ever have to do

But watching you break yourself
Like the way you broke me
Will always hurt

But at least now
You won't be hurting me

Against the Rays

It's the long nights
That make the sun
Feel like it's against us

...

I remember when I got butterflies
Waiting outside your door, ready to knock

Now I stare at my phone
Waiting for three dots...

Bad Day

You're not the only one having a bad day
Because when I walk down the street
I look at strangers with begging eyes hoping they'd say hey

For a glimpse of hope that someone wants
What I have to offer

Because when I think about feeling wanted
I think about a Tuesday afternoon

One that's grey or one that's blue or one with a bright,
shining moon
The description of the day truly doesn't matter

Because I always feel the same
A little bit happy, but it only ends sadder

Than the day before when I had a little hope
That when I was walking down the street
A stranger would look at me and say
A word, a line, anything that would end with hey

Feeling Left Out

When I think about feeling left out
I think about the times I am asked to hang out
The excitement immediately rises
And my extrovert pops out

Thinking it is finally
Going to be okay
My friends asked me to come out and play
But little did I know
The sidelines are where I reside

Seeing everyone move forward while
I can't make a step
In the right direction

Because

Maybe I wasn't left out today
But even though I was asked to come out
And play
I am still stuck in my head
Thinking I will fit in
But just not today

Letting You Down

Good enough
Is a phrase I like to
Never describe myself as

Because even though I may be
Good enough
The only thing you look for
Is perfect in your eyes

And as this world turns
So does your head
Passing me by
Each time a word is said

From my mouth
Through your ears
No matter how hard I try
No matter the years

I finally realized
That you never described me as

Good enough

A Good Day

The sun is shining
The birds are chirping
The wind is singing

All the recipes to make
A good day

But that is not why
I smile today

Today is good because
I feel good
I feel free

It's not because I left you
Or you left me

But rather that I feel something
I haven't felt before
I finally feel like me

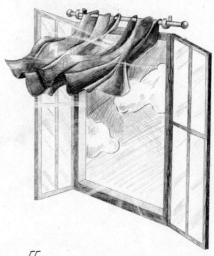

Feeling Complete

To be yourself
And to not need
Anything else

No envy
No hatred
It's just you

Shh the World Is Turning

A silent world we live in
One with loud opinions
And quiet hearts

A world that criticizes your words
And leaves you unheard
To hold your breath
Is a good start

Because in order to make it here
You need to have
An already-broken heart

Click Away Happiness

With a click of a mouse
Or a tap of a finger
No matter the feeling

It always tends to linger

And fade over time
Because the feeling wasn't mine
As the dollars lessen
So does my mind

Losing A Best Friend

I want to ask you if you're doing okay
But I am scared that the answer
Might have to do with me in some way

In a way that I don't want to hear
A message that is messy would eventually turn clear
To understand why you truly left
And that's because you didn't need me

...and I am still here

M & U

I am missing you
But I wish I didn't

I can taste the bitterness
Of your coffee
From when I used to sit
Across the table

Hoping you'd glimpse at me
Wondering if I was able
To brew you another pot
Of the coffee that you love

To make you feel satisfied
And hope that you might
Fall in love again
So I never have to try

And be like this coffee
That you always truly loved

Mask On

While the world protects themselves
From a deadly virus

I protect myself
From being seen

What Is Grief?
Denial, Anger, Bargaining, Depression & Acceptance

I refuse to believe
The pain that I caused
That made you leave

Now every time I look
In the mirror
I hate to see what you left

Can I be happy without you?
After everything we have been through?
Maybe if only I loved you more
Walking away wouldn't be so easy

Maybe it was me
I have been broken for so long
And you ran out of tools
To fix me

But toys are sold in pieces
Which means I'm not broken
I just need to be
Put back together once again

Talking to New People

New people are hard to trust
One moment they give you this feeling
An urge, a rush
And the next thing you know

You're left in the dust

Call Me When You Wake

As your sun rises
Mine always seems to fade
Away with another day
That ends with no words to say

The distance has left me speechless
I miss holding you in my arms
I miss feeling your heartbeat next to mine
I miss our morning coffees and
I miss you

But hearing your voice is still my weakness

So call me when you wake up
It may mean nothing to you
But I need this

I Dropped My Phone

I had this dream
That wakes me often
Of you jumping out of my arms
And off the ledge

Not stopping, not hesitating, not looking back
Just pure courage
And it breaks everything that I am

I am just glad that it was my phone
And not truly you
Because that is a pain
No one can prepare me for

Close but So Far

I never thought I would miss the smell
Of coffee from your mouth
On a cold spring day

Or the times I got mad when you left
Your toothbrush on the counter
Every morning when I awoke

But now that you're not here
Those seem to be the things
That I miss the most

Because not having you here
Hurts a hell of a lot more
Than the distance between us

When I Think of My Mother

When I think of my mother
I think of a cold summer day
One with a little wind and a little rain
A day where we wish the pain
Would just all go away

And it may seem sad, but
When I think of her on a rainy day
I can hear every single person
In the room complaining left and right

As she sits there with a smile on her face
Looking like everything is fine and
We will all be all right

I feel strength and compassion
That no journey is too long and
No battle is too hard

When I think of my mother
I feel happiness, I feel hope
I feel like I am in a world where I belong

Always Sad

Days pass without feeling
Suns rise without being seen
And we live without living

What a vicious cycle it may seem

You're Not Special

You're not special
Not in the sense
That you don't belong
Or that you are worthless

But because you believed me
When you read this

Appreciating Yourself

It is not about the times
You gave up
It is not about the times
You got up

But it is the amount of times
You show up

Confusion of Love

Everything you've ever wanted
Right in front of you
Yet we search for more
To fill the void of loneliness

Complaining and pouting all around
As if love isn't right beside us
At all times, but we fail to acknowledge
Where we belong and we continue

To search for something we
Had all along

The Moment

It all happened so quickly
One moment you are living it
And the next you are reminiscing

Praying for the feeling
To come back again

To feel what was lost
And change up your life
At any cost

Suffering in silence
Picturing it all in your head
Wishing it would all come back
But these moments are dead

And they make room
For new ones to come
But you are stuck thinking
And it has left you feeling numb

Love Just Fits

The common question of
How do I know she's the one?
Has left many men feeling
Like they have never won

As they look at women as prizes
Their future begins to fade
Away into the next lifetime

As they say to themselves
Ah, I'll get her next time

Knock Knock

I was never the problem
But you chose your reason
And you left

When you come back
And knock on that door
Don't be surprised when
It goes silent

Because I am not there
For you anymore

Teapot

To simplify life for you
Imagine a teapot
How steaming hot it is
And how oddly cold it can get

Now it may sound silly
And frankly quite a bit odd
But as life goes on
We lose our heat

That we once started out with
Because as we let people
Distract us from who we
Are meant to be

Our pot goes cold
And we need to take our time
To allow ourselves to reheat

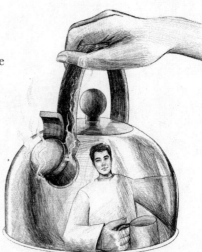

Silence

You always told me
What you never wanted
To hear for yourself

Dreaming with My Eyes Wide Open

There's no time for sleep
There's no time for rest
I dream while I'm awake

Because while the world is sleeping
I'm out trying my best
To fit into this world
Until

I realize that I am unlike the rest

What I Miss Most

From the first day I met you
You felt like a familiar face

We used to swing together as kids
Skip class together as teens
And fall in love by the beach

Even when everyone was around me
You were the one I would miss
Because this isn't the first time we are meeting

You were the one all the dreams were about
The girl that I would one day love

That Hollywood Type of Love

It's the one they talk about in the movies
Where the guy gets the girl
And everything goes so smoothly

There may have been some bumps
But they always got through it
And it always seemed to soothe me

To watch strangers fall in love
And spend a lifetime together
Hoping that my day will come
And I'll find my Heather

Because I never saw the flaws
In the Hollywood relationships
I thought they were easy and simple
Never put together that they
Were holding up scripts

To make it seem true
That love wasn't just something
That was all out of the blue

They convinced me that it was easy
And this girl I dreamt about
Would come by and try to please me

But no one came by
No one even batted an eye
The next version of love I saw
Was in another Hollywood movie
Between just another girl
And just another guy

To My Future Self

No matter where you are
In your life or in the world
Just know that in this moment

You were content
You were proud
You were strong

You were scared
You were lost
You were confused

But most importantly
You were present
And that, my friend,
Is what it's all about

Happy Realization

The happiest I have ever been
Is when the day finally comes to an end
And I can't sleep

Because excitement never rests easy

You Are Here

The silence left before a phrase
Tends to be awkward

But that moment of breath
Is a brief second where
You realize that you are here

82

To Feel Whole

The void we all speak of
Is commonly known
Yet it remains empty
As we continue through life

Trying to find the piece
That fills the hole
To make us feel normal again

The sad truth tends to be
That the hole will never be filled
Because it was never missing
As what we feel is
Not always what we are

The Wake Up

I daydream about the moment
That I wake up and feel peace

The only way to truly experience this
Is to somehow be able to fall asleep

She Kept Moving

Hit after hit
Bruise after bruise
Tear after tear

No matter what life threw
She kept moving on
Without any fear

Because as time went on
So did she
Her wounds healed
Her passion grew
And her strength built
To walk again

And so she did

Difficult to Give Up

The end is so near
And it walks alongside
Of where we are going

Yet we choose to move
Forward in our lives
To show that we are strong
And the end isn't
For very long

The End

As our light begins to fade
A lot of us see a new future
One with brighter skies
And greener grass

One where life just goes
A little smoother

In hopes that a second chance is to come
So that we can continue to live this life
As our first trial run

A Note To Myself

I began writing this book September 22, 2020 and finished May 4, 2021. A poetry book would be easy, they said, it would be quick, they said... but no one accounted for the amount of feelings you have to experience in a year to be able to condense it into a few instalments. Over this past year, I have learned that self-doubt is our biggest barrier because it comes before other people's judgment; it comes before finishing the first page, and before finishing the last page. Self-doubt starts at the root and battles us every step of the way, making us question who we are and why we are doing it.

So when you look back at this book, I want you to understand that this took time, this took effort, and it was damn well worth it. And twenty years from now, I hope you stumble upon this page and realize that this helped a lot of people with their thoughts when they seemed to be all alone. This may seem very conceited to write, and I am not trying to boost my own ego, but I believe we all deserve positive encouragement, even if it is to ourselves. Don't give up before you try; you got this.

Love, j